SEVEN SIMPLE STEPS OF
FINDING *a* MATE
GOD'S WAY

Seven Simple Steps of FINDING *a* MATE GOD'S WAY

USING GOD'S WORD TO FIND THE ONE GOD HAS FOR YOU

GREGORY BACKMON

CREATION
HOUSE

_____

This Book Belongs to

_____

The Day I Received Christ into My Life

_____

The Name of My Church

_____

Date of Purchase

Seven Simple Steps of Finding a Mate God's Way by
Gregory Backmon
Published by Creation House
A Charisma Media Company
600 Rinehart Road
Lake Mary, Florida 32746
www.charismamedia.com

Unless otherwise noted, all Scripture quotations are from are
from the King James Version of the Bible.

Scripture quotations marked AMP are from the Amplified
Bible. Old Testament copyright © 1965, 1987 by the
Zondervan Corporation. The Amplified New Testament
copyright © 1954, 1958, 1987 by the Lockman Foundation.
Used by permission.

Scripture quotations marked THE MESSAGE are from *The
Message: The Bible in Contemporary English*, copyright ©
1993, 1994, 1995, 1996, 2000, 2001, 2002. Used by permission
of NavPress Publishing Group.

All English and Hebrew definitions courtesy of *Vine's
Expository Dictionary*, *Brown-Driver Briggs Hebrew Lexicon*
(abridged), *Strong's Greek/Hebrew Concordance*, and *Thayer's
Greek Lexicon* (abridged), and *Merriam-Webster's Collegiate
Dictionary, Eleventh Edition*.

Design Director: Bill Johnson
Cover design by Terry Clifton

Visit the author by e-mail: gregorybackmon@att.net

Library of Congress Cataloging-in-Publication Data:
2012948811
International Standard Book Number: 978-1-62136-311-8
E-book International Standard Book Number:
978-1-62136-312-5

First edition

12 13 14 15 16 — 987654321
Printed in Canada

DEDICATION

*I dedicate this book to all of my brothers
and sisters in Christ Jesus who are
looking for that special, godly person.
This book is designed to help you to avoid
the pitfalls and traps of the enemy by
making you aware of what to look for
when desiring a potential mate, someone
that you would like to spend the rest
of your life with. It has been said that
you will have to go through a few bad
dates or relationships in order to find
a good one, but that's not true at all,
ladies and gentlemen. That's the way
the world thinks and how they do things
and see things, but that's not how we
as Christians see things. It is not God's
plan for you to go through multiple
relationships in order to find the right
guy or the right girl. It is God's will
that you find the right one the first time
around. God doesn't want His children to
go through the pain, the heartache, the
disappointment, the abuse of a man or
woman in any relationship that is not the
will of God. This book will give you both
spiritual and natural wisdom that you
can apply to your life as you read and
study it. I pray that this book will be an
eye opener and a blessing to you
as you read it.*

ACKNOWLEDGMENTS

I N DEVELOPING THE idea for this book, I would like to give thanks to my Lord and Savior Jesus Christ, and the power of the Holy Spirit Who is at work in me and in all the earth. Secondly, to my beautiful wife Ghislaine, and to all my covenant prayer partners, especially Kenneth and Gloria Copeland who have impacted my life concerning the things of God.

CONTENTS

INTRODUCTION

THERE ARE MANY lonely and single Christian men and women out there who are looking for the right mate and who are tired of dating people that end up a disaster or a nightmare. Don't give up hope; I have some good news for you. This book that you have in your hands will save you time, heartache, pain, and regret. You don't have to run from individual to individual wondering if he or she is for you. After reading this book you will be able to appropriately discern if that man or woman is the one for you without wasting a whole lot of time and even years with that person.

It is God's will that you are joined to the right mate the first time around. If you surrender your heart to God and allow yourself to be led by the Spirit of God, governing your life according to the Word of God, you can't go wrong. God will lead you to your soul mate. You won't have to wonder; you will know!

The purpose of this book is to change the way you think so that you can go about the right and healthy way of dating in a godly fashion. Its purpose is to change you, not your partner or the other person whom you are interested in. If you are currently dating or in a seriously relationship, this book can do two things for you. It can bring your relationship to a whole new level and prep you for marriage, or it can tell you that this person is not the one for you.

If you are a single women or a single man, this book is for you. My advice to you is that you read and study this book before you venture out. Take all the time you need, and don't be in a rush to get into a relationship; don't feel pressured by anyone that you need to have someone now. Wait on God and be led by the Holy Spirit.

You might be saying to yourself, "I have tried everything within my power to find the right person. I have tried blind dating, my friends tried to hook me up with their friends or relatives, I tried online dating, and I tried dating someone from my church and from my job." Finding a mate is not that hard or complicated. God is not a complicated God. He is very simple and practical. We make it hard because we don't want to do things His way, or we allowed the world and other things to influence us instead of being influenced by the Word of God and the Spirit of God. The Bible says that the Spirit is here to help us and to guide us into all truth and that the Word of God is a lamp under our feet and a light to our path.

Step One

ESTABLISHING YOUR FOUNDATION

WHEN PERUSING FOR a potential mate one must first lay down a good and a well-established foundation. This is where the problem lies with single women and men and those that are currently in a relationship. They are pursuing without a foundation, which is the Word of God, and they wonder why their relationships always end up in one disaster after another, dating jerks, fools, and Dr. Jekyll and Mr. Hyde. (For those who don't know about the book and movies based on it, the story of Dr. Jekyll and Mr. Hyde is an old classic about a good doctor whose medical experiment goes wrong and causes him to have dual personalities—one's essence is good but at night the other side of him comes out, which is evil or bad.)

Jesus says in Matthew 7:24–27:

> So everyone who hears these words of Mine and acts upon them [obeying them] will be like a sensible (prudent, practical, wise) man who built his house upon the rock. And the rain fell and the floods came and the winds blew and beat against that house; yet it did not fall, because it had been founded on the rock. And everyone who hears these words of Mine and does not do them will be like a stupid (foolish) man who built his house upon the sand. And the rain fell and the floods came and the

> winds blew and beat against that house, and it fell—
> and great and complete was the fall of it. (AMP)

Notice how the storm hit both houses? The house represents you—one house stood against the storm, and the other didn't. Why? Because that house was built upon a Rock, which is the Word of the living God. Notice what happened to the house that was built on sand; it fell apart. The sand represents things outside the Word of God. It represents the flesh, and when we go after the flesh we are bound to fall. Seeking a mate without building on the Word of God is like a stupid, foolish man. Everything we do must be built and centered on the Word of God. Anything that is built outside the Word of God is going to fall; and you wonder why your relationships fail time after time. It's time to give God a chance. It's time to get God involved. It's time to do it God's way and reap His result in looking for a mate. People think that God is only concerned about our spiritual needs or things, but that's not true. God is concerned about everything that concerns us, even the hair on our head, the Bible says. If God cares about the birds of the air and the Scriptures say that we are much better than the birds of the air, how much should God care about you?

The Bible says, "It's not good that man should be alone" (Gen. 2:18, NKJV). The word for *alone* means "bad" in Hebrew, which means "by themselves, to be separate or isolated." The word *man* applies to females as well as males.

Every man and every woman desires the perfect mate, the man or woman of their dreams. The truth is there is no such thing as a perfect mate. It's a myth. We would all like to think so, but in reality there is not.

God created all of us with different personality traits and characteristics. Each individual has his or her own unique makeup. Essentially, you are the only one of your kind; you will never find anyone like you in this lifetime, nor in that which is to come. The primary question of humanity, with its varying personalities, characteristics, backgrounds, cultures, upbringings, and environments is, How can I choose a mate, or how can I tell whether or not that person is right for me?

The answer is quite simple. As Christians we must seek God and His Word to determine His will as it relates to our mate. God knows the heart and character of each person on the face of the Earth. He knows our motives, our trains of thought, and the manner in which we treat others. God even knows if that individual will be a blessing or a curse to you. God desires for you to be joined to someone who has His own heart and is ultimately seeking His plan. God, your heavenly Father, wants to select your mate. He wants to get involved if you'll let Him, because there are many deceivers and charmers in the midst of us.

The term *charmer* refers to anyone who pretends to be what you're looking for. Some have called them "smooth talkers." They say just what you want to hear and do what makes you feel good at that moment until they get what they want from you. At that point you are no longer a benefit or asset to them; they inconsiderately discard you or they want to become "friends with benefits," if you know what I mean. Those who deceive may even pretend to have your best interests at heart, but only for a season. After that they reveal their true personality and plans. Eventually you will begin to see that person for who he or she is. The sign will be made evident.

However, it is your responsibility to take heed once God reveals these warnings to you. If you are sensitive to the Spirit of God and in tune with the Word of God, God will lead you accordingly, but you have to be ready to obey His leading. When pursuing or waiting for a mate, make the Word of God your barometer. Never depend solely upon the opinions and recommendations of others. It is difficult for us to see another individual's heart. God looks at the heart, but man looks at the outward appearance. (See 1 Samuel 16:7.)

Sometimes friends and/or relatives attempt to play matchmaker, and now we have Internet dating. I'm not knocking Internet dating. There have been some success stories that came from Internet dating. Whether it's friends, relatives, or the Internet, they are all restricted, because they can only base their selection on what they see. Once the truth is revealed you hear statements like, "I didn't know that person was like that," or, "If I had known that person was like that, I never would have set you up with him or her."

Don't make your selection based upon how an individual looks, what kind of job he or she has, how much money the individual makes and how much money they can spend on you, his or her level of success, or his or her social status. There is nothing wrong with those things, but again, God's Word should be your foundation when seeking a mate, just like everything else. If you can seek and acknowledge God concerning His will in what you should be doing in your ministry, career, what church you should join, and how much you should give to this ministry, you should also seek and acknowledge God regarding who you should be dating. He will show you.

If the person whom you are presently considering is not living according to God's standards or pursuing a lifestyle pleasing to God, then God has not ordained the relationship, but the enemy (the devil) may be orchestrating his plan. Salvation should always be a prerequisite before entering a relationship. As Christians we must remember that God loves everyone. However, He is not Father or Lord to every individual born into the Earth. He is only Father and Lord to those who have accepted Jesus in their heart as Lord and Savior.

But you are not living the life of the flesh, you are living the life of the Spirit, if the [Holy] Spirit of God [really] dwells within you [directs and controls you]. But if anyone does not possess the [Holy] Spirit of Christ, he is none of His [he does not belong to Christ, is not truly a child of God].

—ROMANS 8:9, AMP

As a born-again believer it is essential to seek the face of God, read His Word, and pray that every aspect of your life is in accordance with His will. Selecting a mate is no exception. God's desire is for you to be equally yoked to someone who serves the same God you serve and worship, someone who prays to the same God you pray to, and lives by the same principles, laws, and commandments that you live by. Doing things God's way in selecting a mate will ensure your success and eliminate unnecessary stress. Keep in mind that without a firm foundation you won't have much success in finding that right person that God has for you or in your relationship. Let's delve into the Word of God to get His perspective on finding a mate! Are you ready?

SCRIPTURE REFERENCE ON ESTABLISHING YOUR FOUNDATION

Meditate on these scriptures:

Roll your works upon the Lord [commit and trust them wholly to Him; He will cause your thoughts to become agreeable to His will, and] so shall your plans be established and succeed.

—PROVERBS 16:3, AMP

Every purpose is established by counsel: and with good advice make war.

—PROVERBS 20:18

Ponder the path of thy feet, and let all thy ways be established.

—Proverbs 4:26

Without counsel purposes are disappointed: but in the multitude of counsellors they are established.

—Proverbs 15:22

He brought me up also out of an horrible pit, out of the miry clay, and set my feet upon a rock, and established my goings.

—Psalm 40:2

And the head of Ephraim is Samaria, and the head of Samaria is Remaliah's son. If ye will not believe, surely ye shall not be established.

—Isaiah 7:9

Except the Lord build the house, they labour in vain that build it: except the Lord keep the city, the watchman waketh but in vain.

—Psalm 127:1

Step Two

ACKNOWLEDGE GOD
WHEN SEEKING A MATE

GOD HAS ESTABLISHED the criteria for finding a mate. It is outlined in the Word of God. Seven simple steps are listed in this book to ensure God's results in searching for a godly mate. We said that step one was to establish your foundation. Without a foundation you cannot build a solid relationship, and it starts with the Word. The Word of God is our foundation; it is our support system. The second step is that we must acknowledge God no matter what.

> Trust in the Lord with all thine heart; and lean not unto thine own understanding. In all thy ways acknowledge him, and he shall direct thy paths.
> —PROVERBS 3:5–6

I like what the Amplified Bible and *The Message* Bible read:

> Lean on, trust in, and be confident in the Lord with all your heart and mind and do not rely on your own insight or understanding. In all your ways know, recognize, and acknowledge Him, and He will direct and make straight and plain your paths.
> —PROVERBS 3:5–6, AMP

> Trust God from the bottom of your heart; don't try to figure out everything on your own. Listen for God's voice in everything you do, everywhere you go; he's the one who will keep you on track.
>
> —Proverbs 3:5–6, The Message

The aforementioned Scripture passage encourages us not to rely on our own reasoning or understanding but to trust God with all of our heart. Unfortunately we, as humans, would rather trust and give our heart to another man or woman. Then we wonder why our relationships are not fruitful and productive. The Bible admonishes us to continuously trust God with all our hearts.

To trust in yourself or to rely on your own heart and mind will lead you to destruction in the long run. Remember that you are not smarter or wiser than God, so why not trust Him instead? Proverbs 14:12 (AMP) says, "There is a way which seems right to a man and appears straight before him, but at the end of it is the way of death."

"In other words, you're saying that I know what I am doing; I don't need God's help? Besides that, I am smart and well educated to make my own decision." Your decision without God can and will lead you to your death, as it is stated in Proverbs 14:12. The word *death* there (*maveth* in Hebrew) means "ruin," which means "complete failure, complete devastation." We all have been there—some more than others—but all that can change now. You don't have to go through that anymore.

That's why Proverbs 3:6 admonishes us to acknowledge God in all we do. This includes the process of finding a mate. It is only when we choose to obey and acknowledge God by acknowledging His Word that He directs our paths. In other words, God will order your steps and direct you to the right individual that He has for you, that special someone who will be just what you need, at the right time and place.

Oftentimes when we allow God to select a mate for us it is not the person we expect. We would choose someone based upon his or her physical features, hair texture, economic status, skin tone, educational level, and possessions. Granted, there is nothing wrong with possessing these things; but we falter when we make these things our top priority. We allow these outward appearances and material things to cloud our vision and cause us to lose focus on seeking God to know the contents of an individual's heart. Only God knows the heart of every man. We can fool each other, but we cannot fool God.

> But the LORD said unto Samuel, Look not on his countenance, or on the height of his stature; because I have refused him: for the LORD seeth not as man seeth; for man looketh on the outward appearance, but the LORD looketh on the heart.
>
> —1 SAMUEL 16:7

Let's read this verse from the Amplified Bible and from *The Message* Bible.

The Amplified Bible reads:

> But the Lord said to Samuel, Look not on his appearance or at the height of his stature, for I have rejected him. For the Lord sees not as man sees; for man looks on the outward appearance, but the Lord looks on the heart.

The Message Bible reads:

> But GOD told Samuel, "Looks aren't everything. Don't be impressed with his looks and stature. I've already eliminated him. GOD judges persons differently than humans do. Men and women look at the face; GOD looks into the heart."

God says, "I have rejected him." God has rejected or eliminated the individual that you have your heart and eyes on, but for some reason you still want to be with that person. When we choose a mate based solely on what we see, our failure is certain. We end up getting hurt and disappointed. The first thing we do? We blame God for the mess that we are in, saying, "Why, Lord, why did You let this happen to me?"

We must guard our heart and harness our emotions. Let's us take heed to the Spirit of God and the Word of God, lest we fall head over heels with a mirage, something that appears to be there when in all actuality it is not what you want or what you are looking for. A seemingly nice personality or a few good dates is not sufficient evidence to make a conclusion to marry or even talking about getting married. The Bible tells us to be wise. (See Matthew 10:16.)

When you take that mate as your husband or wife your destiny becomes tied into the destiny of that individual. For this reason it is essential that you get involved with someone that God has for you. If you choose to marry or get involved with a thug; drug dealer; thief; or someone who is uncommitted, having multiple partners; someone who has no regard for God's standards, purpose, or plan for their life but seeks to consume alcohol and live a life of partying excessively and living riotously, you become part-owner of that destiny.

If this is what you desire in a mate, continue to do what you are doing, pursuing your own way despite God's ways. Continuing to fail to acknowledge God in all your ways will lead to disaster. This is why so many people, even Christians—especially women—fall into the hands of abusers of all kinds. They fail to acknowledge God. The word *acknowledge* in Hebrew is *yada,* which means "to recognize, to consider." In other words, you must include God in everything that you do. That also means finding a suitable mate, so make it a priority to pursue your mate with God's purpose in mind. Desire an individual who has a wonderful relationship with God and is following God's plans for his or her life. God's ordained destiny will be manifested in both of your lives, and your relationship and your marriage will be fulfilling, naturally and spiritually. People want God to direct their path, but how can He if they don't acknowledge Him? In order for God to direct anyone's path they must acknowledge Him first. Many times we make the decision first without God, and when things don't work out then we go to God. Go to God first and ask Him what you should do, and He will direct your path. That's His promise to you.

To acknowledge God is like acknowledging the doctor before you try any new diet pills that just came out on the market or going to a good mechanic before you buy that used car to see what they say. The mechanic might tell you, "Don't buy this car, because the car is not worth getting. The body looks good, the inside looks good, the tires look good, but the motor is bad. It needs work, major work." You see how that mechanic saves you time, money, and a headache and keeps you from being stranded on the freeway or in the middle of nowhere. God is the same way. If you will take the time to acknowledge Him, He will save you time, money, years, and heartache. Don't say that you don't have time. You do. Make time or else suffer the consequence for not including God.

SCRIPTURE REFERENCE ON ACKNOWLEDGING GOD

Meditate on these scriptures:

> Trust in the Lord with all thine heart; and lean not unto thine own understanding. In all thy ways acknowledge him, and he shall direct thy paths.
> —PROVERBS 3:5–6

11

Then they told David, saying, Behold, the Philistines fight against Keilah, and they rob the threshingfloors. Therefore David enquired of the Lord, saying, Shall I go and smite these Philistines? And the Lord said unto David, Go, and smite the Philistines, and save Keilah. And David's men said unto him, Behold, we be afraid here in Judah: how much more then if we come to Keilah against the armies of the Philistines? Then David enquired of the Lord yet again. And the Lord answered him and said, Arise, go down to Keilah; for I will deliver the Philistines into thine hand.

—1 Samuel 23:1–4

And David enquired at the Lord, saying, Shall I pursue after this troop? shall I overtake them? And he answered him, Pursue: for thou shalt surely overtake them, and without fail recover all.

—1 Samuel 30:8

And the children of Israel enquired of the Lord, (for the ark of the covenant of God was there in those days.

—Judges 20:27

Enquire, I pray thee, of the Lord for us; for Nebuchadrezzar king of Babylon maketh war against us; if so be that the Lord will deal with us according to all his wondrous works, that he may go up from us.

—Jeremiah 21:2

And David enquired of God, saying, Shall I go up against the Philistines? And wilt thou deliver them into mine hand? And the Lord said unto him, Go up; for I will deliver them into thine hand.

—1 Chronicles 14:10

Step Three

PUT ALL YOUR ENERGY AND TIME INTO SEEKING GOD FOR A MATE

Therefore I say unto you, Take no thought for your life, what ye shall eat, or what ye shall drink; nor yet for your body, what ye shall put on. Is not the life more than meat, and the body than raiment? Behold the fowls of the air: for they sow not, neither do they reap, nor gather into barns; yet your heavenly Father feedeth them. Are ye not much better than they? Which of you by taking thought can add one cubit unto his stature? And why take ye thought for raiment? Consider the lilies of the field, how they grow; they toil not, neither do they spin: And yet I say unto you, That even Solomon in all his glory was not arrayed like one of these. Wherefore, if God so clothe the grass of the field, which to day is, and to morrow is cast into the oven, shall he not much more clothe you, O ye of little faith? Therefore take no thought, saying, What shall we eat? or, What shall we drink? or, Wherewithal shall we be clothed? (For after all these things do the Gentiles seek:) for your heavenly Father knoweth that ye have need of all these things. But seek ye first the kingdom of God, and his righteousness; and all these things shall be added unto you.

—MATTHEW 6:25–33

I N MATTHEW 6:26, it says that God cares for the birds of the air, and that you are much better than them. Now, if God cares for the birds and feedeth them, how much more does God care about you and whom you date? God doesn't want you to be lonely. He created you to be with someone of His choice. All you have to do is obey what Matthew 6:33 says, "But seek ye first the kingdom of God, and his righteousness; and all these things shall be added unto you."

Notice it says "first," but we've got it backward; we want to put God second or last. The word *first* means "above all things." The word *first* also means "to start with, to begin with, the most important, primary, top priority." The word *seek* means "to aim at, strive after, require, to crave. To seek in order to find out by thinking, meditating, reasoning, to enquire into, to go about, desire." It also mean to research. The question is, Are you making God your top priority, or are you making that man or that woman whom you are seeking your top priority? There is nothing wrong with seeking, but seeking a mate without putting God and His Word first is the problem that most single Christian people have.

According to Matthew 6:33, God wants you to pursue Him first. He wants you to pursue His kingdom and His righteousness, which means His way of doing and being right, and everything else will fall in place or be added unto you. When you put God first and pursue Him with all of your heart, all that added stuff will come—the house, the car, the man or the woman of your dreams will show up— all because you decided to put God first. When you put God first He will put you first.

Unfortunately too many people, especially Christian women, spend the majority of their time looking for others to fill the void of loneliness in their lives instead of seeking the Source of all creation, God Almighty. Many feel the urgency to enter into relationships because they believe that their time is running out due to age, all of their friends are married or getting married, or because they are feeling lonely and have been single for a long time. None of these reasons are good enough to cause you to take your eyes off of God and search out benefits for yourself. By fulfilling your own desire or pursuing your own lusts you become a primary target for the enemy, and believe me, you don't want that.

The enemy's main goal is to steal, kill, and destroy. He will sidetrack you from God's plan for your life and who God has for you. The devil will tell you that God has forgotten about you, and that's why you are still lonely or not married. He will put thoughts and ideas in your head, like, "All the good ones are taken or gay, and therefore you must settle for less." He will cause you to go after the married ones and say it is of God. I have seen some Christian women dating married men all because of how they were being treated, insecure in themselves, battling with loneliness, and out of desperation. There is no future in someone who is married. That married man or woman will not leave their family for you, especially if they have established a lot together. All you are getting is an empty promise that he or she will leave their spouse and have you waiting, wasting your time and years in something that is not going to happen. You have put all of your heart, soul, and body into this relationship that will never be what God has created it to be—days of heaven on Earth. There have been some Christians dating men and women that were married and didn't even know it until months or years later, all because they did not seek God. Now they are hurt and mad with God, saying, "Lord, how could You let this happen to me? Now I'm pregnant by this man," or, "I got this woman pregnant." It wasn't God's fault. You allowed the enemy to come in and deceive you. Thank God we serve a merciful God who is willing to forgive you and put you back on track.

When you take yourself out of God's hand and God's will, you are placing yourself in a vulnerable position, giving the enemy access to come in and bring a counterfeit into your life. Be willing to wait, and earnestly seek God's face to avoid unnecessary hardship. The Bible says, "Let patience have her perfect work" (James 1:4). The word *patience* means "to remain the same until your changes come." The thing is, we live in a microwave society, and so we expect to get everything at the drop of a hat or like instant coffee. God is still God, and His timetable is different from yours. All that is required from you is to wait patiently on Him (Ps. 37:7). It will always be to your advantage to wait for God and allow Him to direct your path.

It is not always going to be easy, but purpose in your heart that you are going to allow God to lead you and guide you. Purpose in your heart that you are going to stop trying to do it yourself and let God be God. God does not need your help. All He needs is your cooperation.

> For we are God's [own] handiwork (His workmanship), recreated in Christ Jesus, [born anew] that we may do those good works which God predestined (planned beforehand) for us [taking paths which He prepared ahead of time], that we should walk in them [living the good life which He prearranged and made ready for us to live].
> —EPHESIANS 2:10, AMP

God already ordained the right individual for you before the foundation of the world. All you have to do is trust Him and exhibit patience. Your heavenly Father knows what's best for you. When you put God first, He will put you first. Remember, God has already prepared and prearranged the good life for you to walk in. God has already prepared and prearranged your mate for you. Your job is to get on the path that God has prearranged for you by getting in the Word, staying in prayer, staying focused, listening to the voice of the Holy Spirit, and exercising faith and patience.

SCRIPTURE REFERENCE ON SEEKING GOD

Meditate on these scriptures:

> With my soul have I desired thee in the night; yea, with my spirit within me will I seek thee early: for when thy judgments are in the earth, the inhabitants of the world will learn righteousness.
>
> —ISAIAH 26:9

> Seek ye the LORD while he may be found, call ye upon him while he is near.
>
> —ISAIAH 55:6

> One thing have I desired of the LORD, that will I seek after; that I may dwell in the house of the LORD all the days of my life, to behold the beauty of the LORD, and to enquire in his temple.
>
> —PSALM 27:4

> The young lions do lack, and suffer hunger: but they that seek the LORD shall not want any good thing.
>
> —PSALM 34:10

> O God, thou art my God; early will I seek thee: my soul thirsteth for thee, my flesh longeth for thee in a dry and thirsty land, where no water is; To see thy power and thy glory, so as I have seen thee in the sanctuary.
>
> —PSALM 63:1–2

> Glory ye in his holy name: let the heart of them rejoice that seek the LORD. Seek the Lord, and his strength: seek his face evermore.
>
> —PSALM 105:3–4

Blessed are they that keep his testimonies, and that seek him with the whole heart.

—Psalm 119:2

But seek ye first the kingdom of God, and his righteousness; and all these things shall be added unto you.

—Matthew 6:33

But without faith it is impossible to please him: for he that cometh to God must believe that he is, and that he is a rewarder of them that diligently seek him.

—Hebrews 11:6

Therefore came I forth to meet thee, diligently to seek thy face, and I have found thee.

—Proverbs 7:15

Step Four

WATCH THE FRUIT THAT IS BEING PRODUCED IN THEIR LIFE

Beware of false prophets, which come to you in sheep's clothing, but inwardly they are ravening wolves. Ye shall know them by their fruits. Do men gather grapes of thorns, or figs of thistles? Even so every good tree bringeth forth good fruit; but a corrupt tree bringeth forth evil fruit. A good tree cannot bring forth evil fruit, neither can a corrupt tree bring forth good fruit. Every tree that bringeth not forth good fruit is hewn down, and cast into the fire. Wherefore by their fruits ye shall know them.

—MATTHEW 7:15–20

IN THIS SCRIPTURE passage, God is not simply warning us about false prophets. This verse can also be apply to people in general, because the world is full of people who will come to you in sheep's clothing, but in their hearts are like wolves, waiting for the opportunity to tear you apart. Jesus says, "Beware." The word *beware* in Greek (*prosecho*) means "to pay attention, be cautious about, to take heed, to watch, to be on guard."

Why must you beware? Because there are many deceivers out there who are ready and waiting to lead you astray. For this reason, you must seek God's direction and provision in all things. Wolves come to devour, stealing all that you have—your time, money, peace, joy, heart—to rob you of your innocence and anything and everything that they can get their hands on. You must take heed to the words of Jesus: beware and watch their fruit, or what is being produced out of their lives. It's not what they say but what they produce; by their fruits you will recognize them.

Jesus says in Matthew 17:20, "Wherefore by their fruits ye shall know them." The fruits that they bear will tell it all. Anyone can talk a good game, but not many can walk the straight and narrow path God has designed for us. As they say, talk is cheap. Action speaks louder than words. What is in that person's heart will be made manifest sooner or later. No one can pretend forever. It's bound to come out. I hope it comes out before you get too involved.

I have two daughters. One of the greatest fears that most fathers have when it comes to their daughters is that they will get involved with guys how we used to be before we came to our senses, and how we used to act in our younger and wild days. We know the games, and there are women that play and know the game too. Those who have been out of the dating game for a while, you are a prime target for the enemy. Don't ever feel and act desperate, because you will surely miss the signs.

First Thessalonians 5:6 says, "Therefore let us not sleep, as do others; but let us watch and be sober." In the game of dating and looking for that right person, you must not sleep, as the Scriptures say. The word *sleep* here means "to yield to sloth and sin." It's like walking around with a blindfold on. When you are asleep all you see are his or her looks, what they can do for you, money, material things, and physique, forgetting all about the fruits that are being manifest in that person's life.

Let's read Matthew 7:15–20 again:

> Beware of false prophets, which come to you in sheep's clothing, but inwardly they are ravening wolves. Ye shall know them by their fruits. Do men gather grapes of thorns, or figs of thistles? Even so every good tree bringeth forth good fruit; but a corrupt tree bringeth forth evil fruit. A good tree cannot bring forth evil fruit, neither can a corrupt tree bring forth good fruit. Every tree that bringeth not forth good fruit is hewn down, and cast into the fire. Wherefore by their fruits ye shall know them.

There are only two types of trees: a good tree and a corrupt tree. The question is, Which tree do you want, the good tree or the bad tree? People are known by the fruit that they bear, and there are lots of people dating corrupt trees. They try to dress it up, they try to cover it up, they try to defend by making excuses why they do the things they do. Let me tell you a secret. The tree that you are dating is corrupt, so stop trying and get out of that mess. Look for a good tree, a tree that is in line with the Word according to Galatians 5:22. The fruit that your mate should be producing is the fruit of the Spirit, not the fruit of the world but of God, which is love, kindness, peace, temperance, goodness, meekness, faith, gentleness, and patience.

If you see that more of the works of the flesh than the Spirit are being manifest in him or her according to Galatians 5:19–21, take heed and flee! Before you get too involved or emotionally attached, take time to ask questions. Find out if they have an authentic, committed relationship with God, studying the Word consistently, attending church services regularly. Ask them about their prayer life and their communing with God on a daily basis. Find out whom they hang around with and the places they go. Watch continuously to monitor their lifestyle not just in church but outside of church as well. The fruit will be evident; the fruit will tell you all that you need to know about that person.

Fruit is like a picture or a video. When someone tries to rob a bank, the first thing the police want to see is the picture or the video footage of that person who's doing the robbery. The picture and the video act as evidence that the man is guilty. So is the fruit that is being produced in the life of the one you are dating. The fruit that you see is your evidence that he or she is the one that is sent by God or by the devil.

SCRIPTURE REFERENCES ON WATCHING THE FRUIT THAT IS BEING PRODUCED OUT OF THEIR LIVES

Meditate on these scriptures:

> Therefore let us not sleep, as do others; but let us watch and be sober.
> —1 THESSALONIANS 5:6

> Beware of dogs, beware of evil workers, beware of the concision.
> —PHILIPPIANS 3:2

> Beware lest any man spoil you through philosophy and vain deceit, after the tradition of men, after the rudiments of the world, and not after Christ.
> —COLOSSIANS 2:8

> But the end of all things is at hand: be ye therefore sober, and watch unto prayer.
> —1 PETER 4:7

Be sober, be vigilant; because your adversary the devil, as a roaring lion, walketh about, seeking whom he may devour.

—1 PETER 5:8

Watch and pray, that ye enter not into temptation: the spirit indeed is willing, but the flesh is weak.

—MATTHEW 26:41

Beware of false prophets, which come to you in sheep's clothing, but inwardly they are ravening wolves. Ye shall know them by their fruits. Do men gather grapes of thorns, or figs of thistles? Even so every good tree bringeth forth good fruit; but a corrupt tree bringeth forth evil fruit. A good tree cannot bring forth evil fruit, neither can a corrupt tree bring forth good fruit. Every tree that bringeth not forth good fruit is hewn down, and cast into the fire. Wherefore by their fruits ye shall know them.

—MATTHEW 7:15–20

And no marvel; for Satan himself is transformed into an angel of light.

—2 CORINTHIANS 11:14

Lest Satan should get an advantage of us: for we are not ignorant of his devices.

—2 CORINTHIANS 2:11

Step Five

DON'T SEEK AN UNBELIEVER (NON-CHRISTIAN) FOR A MATE

Be ye not unequally yoked together with unbelievers: for what fellowship hath righteousness with unrighteousness? and what communion hath light with darkness? And what concord hath Christ with Belial? or what part hath he that believeth with an infidel? And what agreement hath the temple of God with idols? for ye are the temple of the living God; as God hath said, I will dwell in them, and walk in them; and I will be their God, and they shall be my people. Wherefore come out from among them, and be ye separate, saith the Lord, and touch not the unclean thing; and I will receive you. And will be a Father unto you, and ye shall be my sons and daughters, saith the Lord Almighty.

—2 CORINTHIANS 6:14–18

THERE ARE SOME Christians who are in an unequally yoked relationship. What I mean by that is they don't believe the same thing, and that can and will create problems. The Word of God has instructed us not to go after an unbeliever; an unbeliever is someone who is not saved. They haven't given their life to Christ. You can be unequally yoked even if that person is a Christian; if that person just got saved they need some time to be groomed in the Word and in the things of God before you even think about pursuing him or her. Yoking up with a new believer is like yoking up with an unbeliever, because they still have their worldly ways and their mind hasn't been trained and developed yet in the ways of God, and that takes time.

It is so important for Christians that you and your mate believe in the same thing when it comes to the Word of God. The Word of God will only work when you and your mate are in agreement with one other. For example, one might believe in tithing and the other one might not believe in tithing. One might believe in speaking in tongues and operating in the supernatural gifts, and the other one might not believe in that. Some Christians believe that God wants us to prosper, and some Christians don't believe that God wants us to prosper. There are some who really believe and practice holiness and some don't.

The first thing you should ask when dating or if someone introduces you to someone is, "Are you saved?" If the answer is no, tell them in a nice and godly way, "No thank you." If the answer is yes, ask how long he or she has been saved, what church they attend, and how often they attend church. In other words, do your homework on them. Find out all you can about them.

Ladies, don't let the devil trick you into thinking that there are no godly men in the church and that all men are the same. That's not true at all. But, I must admit that there are men in the church that act like worldly men. On the other hand, there are men that really love God and are living for God.

In 2 Corinthians 6:14–18 God warns Christians not to get in involved with unsaved people. That doesn't mean we shouldn't love them. It means that you as a child of God should not be looking for or going after someone who's not saved. It doesn't matter how nice that person is. God has little regard for how nice a person is, if they go to church every Sunday, or even if they are a member of a church; that still doesn't change the fact of what God says in His Word. The Bible says in Romans 8:9, "But ye are not in the flesh, but in the Spirit, if so be that the Spirit of God dwell in you. Now if any man have not the Spirit of Christ, he is none of his."

Let's read this verse from the Amplified Bible for a clearer understanding:

> But you are not living the life of the flesh, you are living the life of the Spirit, if the [Holy] Spirit of God [really] dwells within you [directs and controls you]. But if anyone does not possess the [Holy] Spirit of Christ, he is none of His [he does not belong to Christ, is not truly a child of God].

You have to be saved in order to posses the Spirit of God. If a potential mate is not saved, or born again, we are admonished not to yoke up or pursue a relationship with them. From God's eyes and how He sees it, we are called righteousness, and they are called unrighteousness. We are called light; they are called darkness. We are called Christ; they are called Belial. We are called believers; they are called infidels. We are called the temple of God; they are called idols. Do you see the difference and why God says not to get involved with an unbeliever?

Let's read 2 Corinthians 6:14–18 from the Amplified Bible:

> Do not be unequally yoked with unbelievers [do not make mismated alliances with them or come under a different yoke with them, inconsistent with your faith]. For what partnership have right living and right standing with God with iniquity and lawlessness? Or how can light have fellowship with darkness? What harmony can there be between Christ and Belial [the devil]? Or what has a believer in common with an unbeliever? What agreement [can there be between] a temple of God and idols? For

we are the temple of the living God; even as God said, I will dwell in and with and among them and will walk in and with and among them, and I will be their God, and they shall be My people. So, come out from among [unbelievers], and separate (sever) yourselves from them, says the Lord, and touch not [any] unclean thing; then I will receive you kindly and treat you with favor, And I will be a Father to you, and you shall be My sons and daughters, says the Lord Almighty.

As Christians we live our lives according to God's standards and rules; a non-Christian governs his or her life by Satan's influence and by this world's system. The Bible denotes that we are in the world but not of the world. The unsaved are of this world and are under its influence.

There are so many Christians, especially women, who often go into a relationship with an ungodly person with the preconceived notion that they can change that person. They think that they will get saved as a result of becoming involved with them. That is one of the biggest mistakes that anyone can make. In actuality they are the ones who end up compromising in order to keep that man or that woman in their lives. Unfortunately I have seen so many Christian women who have hastily selected a mate, and they didn't care whether he was saved or not; they just wanted to have someone in their lives or were attempting to soothe their loneliness. Others have selected a mate based upon outward appearances, as we expounded upon earlier in the book.

Remember that being unequally yoked can also be applied to two saved people. Stunted spiritual growth and lack of spiritual development in relation to the Word of God can render an individual incompatible spiritually. Deuteronomy 7:1–4 is a good example of why God doesn't want His children to date or marry an unbeliever:

> When the LORD thy God shall bring thee into the
> land whither thou goest to possess it, and hath cast
> out many nations before thee, the Hittites, and the
> Girgashites, and the Amorites, and the Canaanites,
> and the Perizzites, and the Hivites, and the Jebusites,
> seven nations greater and mightier than thou; And
> when the LORD thy God shall deliver them before
> thee; thou shalt smite them, and utterly destroy
> them; thou shalt make no covenant with them, nor
> shew mercy unto them: Neither shalt thou make
> marriages with them; thy daughter thou shalt not
> give unto his son, nor his daughter shalt thou take
> unto thy son. For they will turn away thy son from
> following me, that they may serve other gods: so
> will the anger of the LORD be kindled against you,
> and destroy thee suddenly.

This scripture is so full of spiritual truth. It even applies
to us today. The Hittites, Girgashites, Amorites, Canaanites,
Perizzites, Hivites, and the Jebusites were people who didn't
have a covenant relationship with God. They were ungodly
people, serving the devil. When God's people get involved
with the Hittites, Girgashites, Amorites, Canaanites,
Perizzites, Hivites, and the Jebusites, people who do not have
a covenant relationship with God, you open the door for
Satan to work his will, and that is to kill, steal, and to destroy.
I have seen when God's people got involved with ungodly
people and backslid. They were back in the clubs, drinking
and smoking. They walk out of God's plans and purpose for
their life. They quit going to church, stop reading their Bible.
They start dressing and talking different. Why? Because they
did not take heed to the Word of God.

> Neither shalt thou make marriages with them; thy
> daughter thou shalt not give unto his son, nor his

daughter shalt thou take unto thy son. For they will turn away thy son from following me, that they may serve other gods: so will the anger of the LORD be kindled against you, and destroy thee suddenly.

—DEUTERONOMY 7:3–4

You must value your covenant with God, serve God with all of your heart, and reject anything and every relationship that will jeopardize your commitment to God. Don't buy into the lies of the devil that there are no good Christian men or women out there and that they are just as bad as the ungodly ones so that you can go after an ungodly one. It's all a trick. Yes, there are some Christian people that make it hard for others, but don't let that stop you from seeking a godly man or a godly woman. There are some good Christian people out there that are living right and love the Lord with all their heart, but you just have to be patient and let God do it.

SCRIPTURE REFERENCES ON NOT SEEKING AN UNBELIEVER FOR A MATE

Meditate on these scriptures:

And have no fellowship with the unfruitful works of darkness, but rather reprove them.

—EPHESIANS 5:11

Unto the pure all things are pure: but unto them that are defiled and unbelieving is nothing pure; but even their mind and conscience is defiled.

—TITUS 1:15

Be ye not unequally yoked together with unbelievers: for what fellowship hath righteousness with unrighteousness? and what communion hath light with darkness? And what concord hath Christ with

Belial? or what part hath he that believeth with an infidel? And what agreement hath the temple of God with idols? for ye are the temple of the living God; as God hath said, I will dwell in them, and walk in them; and I will be their God, and they shall be my people. Wherefore come out from among them, and be ye separate, saith the Lord, and touch not the unclean thing; and I will receive you. And will be a Father unto you, and ye shall be my sons and daughters, saith the Lord Almighty.

—2 CORINTHIANS 6:14–18

When the LORD thy God shall bring thee into the land whither thou goest to possess it, and hath cast out many nations before thee, the Hittites, and the Girgashites, and the Amorites, and the Canaanites, and the Perizzites, and the Hivites, and the Jebusites, seven nations greater and mightier than thou; And when the LORD thy God shall deliver them before thee; thou shalt smite them, and utterly destroy them; thou shalt make no covenant with them, nor shew mercy unto them: Neither shalt thou make marriages with them; thy daughter thou shalt not give unto his son, nor his daughter shalt thou take unto thy son. For they will turn away thy son from following me, that they may serve other gods: so will the anger of the LORD be kindled against you, and destroy thee suddenly.

—DEUTERONOMY 7:1–4

Blessed is the man that walketh not in the counsel of the ungodly, nor standeth in the way of sinners, nor sitteth in the seat of the scornful.

—PSALM 1:1

Step Six

BE LED BY THE SPIRIT AND NOT YOUR FLESH

For as many as are led by the Spirit of God, they are the sons of God.

—Romans 8:14

THE BIBLE SAYS that those who are led by the Spirit of God are the sons of God. When pursuing a mate, it is imperative that you are led by the Spirit of God and not by man or feeling.

As a Christian, you must learn how to be led by the Spirit of God. You must learn how to allow the Spirit of God to lead your human spirit, the recreated spirit on the inside of you. It is through your spirit that God is going to lead you to your special mate. God is not going to lead you through your flesh. The Bible says that God is going to guide you through your spirit.

What gets us into trouble is our flesh. Following the flesh will cause you to fall short of God's best. The flesh is prone to choose according to the sense realm and not the spirit realm. In other words, the flesh always operates contrary to the Spirit of God and the Word of God. That's why the Bible says in Romans 8:8, "So then they that are in the flesh cannot please God." You might be wondering, What is flesh? The word *flesh* in the Greek, *sarx* or *sarkos*, means "human nature, a way of thinking that opposes the Word and the will of God, the earthly nature of man apart from divine influence, and therefore prone to sin and opposed to God." In other words, if you are not being led or guided by the Spirit of God in your decision, then you are in the flesh, and your decision is going to be based on fleshly desires, which will lead you away from God plan.

The Spirit and the flesh have enmity against one another. Your recreated spirit wants to please God, and your flesh wants to please itself. It still wants to be a part of this world, doing things the way you used to do before you got saved. On the other hand, if you choose to be led by the Spirit, you will not be susceptible to falling for anything or anyone who comes your way.

You will know beyond the shadow of a doubt that the individual is who you need to be with. The Holy Spirit will tell you, "That's the one." You may ask, "How can I be sure that my spirit is leading me correctly?" Good question. The answer is recorded in the Word of God. First John 2:20 states, "But ye have an unction from the Holy One, and ye know all things." As a born-again believer being led by the Spirit of God, you can know all things according to what 1 John 2:20 says. The reason why many of us profess not to know all things is because we have not totally surrendered our spirit to the Holy Spirit, who knows everything and is willing to reveal to you all that God has for you. It is your responsibility to learn how to listen and obey the Spirit of God that lives in you. He is there to lead you and guide you, even from danger.

You have a choice. You can choose to obey your flesh, or you can choose to obey the Spirit of God, which is the Holy Spirit. Always follow the witness of your spirit, not your mind or your feeling. It can and will mislead you every time. You cannot go back and do things the old way, like when you were out there in the world. Your mind-set will have to change. If not you are going to end up doing things you used to do in order to get a mate, and you don't want that. That's why Romans 12:2 says, "And be not conformed to this world: but be ye transformed by the renewing of your mind, that ye may prove what is that good, and acceptable, and perfect, will of God."

I like to read this verse from the Amplified Bible for more clarification:

> Do not be conformed to this world (this age), [fashioned after and adapted to its external, superficial customs], but be transformed (changed) by the [entire] renewal of your mind [by its new ideals and its new attitude], so that you may prove [for yourselves] what is the good and acceptable and perfect will of God, *even* the thing which is good and acceptable and perfect [in His sight for you].
>
> —ROMANS 12:2

Word to the wise: as a Christian don't let people's prophecies over you that so-and-so will be your husband or your wife move you. I don't care if he or she is your pastor; listen to the witness in your spirit by continuously strengthening your spirit man by reading, meditating, fasting, and praying (especially in the Spirit). If people prophesy over you, especially your leader, it should only confirm what God has already put into your heart to do. First John 4:1 says, "Beloved, believe not every spirit, but try the spirits whether they are of God: because many false prophets are gone out into the world." I'm not saying that your pastor or your leader or someone you respect in the gospel is a false prophet. But remember, we are human, and we are capable of missing God at times. Whatever they say and prophesy over you, it should always bear witness with your spirit.

Let me give you an example. It happened in the early nineties. I had heard that my friend was getting married. We were all going to the same church. It was prophesied over her by the pastor and his wife, but I knew instantly in my spirit that he wasn't the one. I tried to warn her without hurting her feelings because of the excitement that she was getting married. She was in my Bible study class, and that night I taught on being led by the Spirit, hoping that she would catch on, because I didn't want to sound like I was going against my leaders.

She married him, and two years later they were divorced. She said to me that she was living in hell. It was over before it got started. But I asked her, "What did your spirit say, that inward witness of the Holy Spirit?" She said to me, "I knew in my heart not to do it, but because it was prophesied over me by my pastors, I married him. But I knew something was wrong." That's why we must be led by the Spirit of God and not by our feelings and emotion. We must put our flesh under subjection to the Spirit and allow the Spirit to control and dominate us. Remember that our flesh is our greatest enemy and that we must take control over our flesh by allowing the Word and the Spirit to dominate or take the driver's seat.

The Bible says that we are led by the Spirit of God—not by men or women of God or our feelings and emotion but by the Spirit—and what they say should be confirming what God has said to you in your private time of prayer. John 16:13 says, "Howbeit when he, the Spirit of truth, is come, he will guide you into all truth: for he shall not speak of himself; but whatsoever he shall hear, that shall he speak: and he will shew you things to come."

The Bible says that the Spirit of truth wants to guide you. He wants to be your personal guide and lead you to the person you're supposed to be with, but if you are insistent on listening to your flesh and what others say, how can the Spirit of God lead you? How can He guide you? How can He speak to your heart when your flesh is in His way? You are going to have to crucify your flesh and put it under subjection in order for the Spirit to lead you and guide you to your mate.

Not only does He want to lead you and guide you, but He also wants to show you things about that person before you get too involved. Let's read that last statement in John 16:13 again. It reads, "...and he will shew you things to come." But you will have to pay attention to what He wants to show you or reveal to you about what others don't know about that person. For instance, the Holy Spirit might be telling you that he or she is still married or has a very bad temper. He or she could be controlling, promiscuous, a gold digger, on drugs or selling drugs, with one foot in the church and the other foot out of the church, not fully sold out to God.

There was a situation that happened years ago in the late nineties. I saw this young woman giving her testimony on TV. She said that she had met this guy, and he was very handsome and nice. He would buy her anything she wanted. They got married and they lived in a very good neighborhood. She said she noticed that her husband traveled a lot out of town. She was thinking that he was a big time salesman, or working for the government because of the lifestyle that they were living. They were married for over ten years, and she had just had found out that he was a professional hit man. He was making a living by killing people; that was his career. She said that all those years living with her husband she had no idea that he was a killer working for the mob. She gave her life to the Lord, and the Lord delivered her and her husband. She said that she was afraid for her life. Once you get involved with the mob it's hard to get out, and oftentimes the only way out is by death. That's why it pays to listen and follow the direction of the Holy Spirit.

You will be surprised how many women are in that same kind of situation or a similar situation. I have friends that are in and have been in situations like that; one of my friends said to me that she regrets ever getting involved with that person. He's in jail serving a life sentence for murder and selling drugs.

This is one of the main reasons why we cannot listen and be motivated by our flesh. The flesh will always lead you wrong. It will lead you away from God's plan and purpose for your life. If you are going to date, please keep that flesh under subjection. Don't make any decision based on your feeling and emotion. Tell your flesh to be quiet and listen closely to what your spirit is saying. Ask yourself these questions: What is God saying about this relationship? Holy Spirit, is this the one for me? Then listen for the answer. If the Holy Spirit prompts you or speaks to you saying, "Don't do it," be quick to obey and leave him or her alone without any hesitation. It might hurt the flesh, but in the end it will be well worth it. So learn to be led by the Spirit and not your flesh. Your flesh is not your friend. It is your worst enemy.

Don't let Satan take advantage of the weakness of your flesh to trap you into making the wrong choice. Be like Paul, who said, "But I keep under my body, and bring it into subjection: lest that by any means, when I have preached to others, I myself should be a castaway" (1 Cor. 9:27). Paul said, "I keep my body under, and I bring my body under subjection." Paul is saying, "I'm not going to let my body control me or tell me what to do, but I'm (the spirit man is) going to control my body and tell it what to do." The only way you can do that is by prayer, fasting, and meditating on the Word of God day and night.

Here is something to think about while you're meditating on the Word. Paying attention to the leading of the Holy Spirit is like paying attention to a traffic light. You have your green light, which means "go"; you have your yellow light, which means "caution, slow down"; and you have your red light, which means "stop." The green light means peace. When you sense the peace of God in your heart it's God saying, "Go ahead. You have My approval." The yellow light means caution. It is saying, "I'm not sure about this person, but at the same time I'll be watching and praying in the spirit until I get some lucidity on the situation." The red light means stop. God is saying, "Don't do it." Don't get involved with that person, and if you are involved, cut it off and do it quickly. And if you are insistent on dating that person you will not have God's approval, and therefore you are wasting your time praying, fasting, and confessing the Word over that relationship.

SCRIPTURE REFERENCE ON BEING LED BY THE SPIRIT

Meditate on the following scriptures:

> The spirit of man is the candle of the LORD, searching all the inward parts of the belly.
> —PROVERBS 20:27

> I will instruct thee and teach thee in the way which thou shalt go: I will guide thee with mine eye.
> —PSALM 32:8

> For as many as are led by the Spirit of God, they are the sons of God.
> —ROMANS 8:14

> Howbeit when he, the Spirit of truth, is come, he will guide you into all truth: for he shall not speak of himself; but whatsoever he shall hear, that shall he speak: and he will shew you things to come.
> —JOHN 16:13

And Jesus being full of the Holy Ghost returned from Jordan, and was led by the Spirit into the wilderness.

—Luke 4:1

Now there were in the church that was at Antioch certain prophets and teachers; as Barnabas, and Simeon that was called Niger, and Lucius of Cyrene, and Manaen, which had been brought up with Herod the tetrarch, and Saul. As they ministered to the Lord, and fasted, the Holy Ghost said, Separate me Barnabas and Saul for the work whereunto I have called them. And when they had fasted and prayed, and laid their hands on them, they sent them away. So they, being sent forth by the Holy Ghost, departed unto Seleucia; and from thence they sailed to Cyprus.

—Acts 13:1–4

Step Seven

DELIGHT YOURSELF
IN THE LORD

Trust in the LORD, and do good; so shalt thou dwell in the land, and verily thou shalt be fed. Delight thyself also in the LORD: and he shall give thee the desires of thine heart.

—PSALM 37:3–4

ONE OF THE quickest ways to getting God to move on your behalf when desiring a mate or anything that your heart desires is to delight yourself in Him. In other words, do not delight yourself in the pursuit of a mate. Instead, delight yourself in God and what He has promised you in His Word. God has given us some wonderful promises in His Word, and what He has promised you He will deliver, so just relax and rejoice in Him.

Nevertheless my lovingkindness will I not utterly take from him, nor suffer my faithfulness to fail. My covenant will I not break, nor alter the thing that is gone out of my lips. Once have I sworn by my holiness that I will not lie unto David.

—PSALM 89:33–35

You can read this verse and make it personal by putting your name in it. "Nevertheless my lovingkindness will I not utterly take from him, nor suffer my faithfulness to fail. My covenant will I not break, nor alter the thing that is gone out of my lips. Once have I sworn by my holiness that I will not lie unto _____." That is enough to delight in and to praise God for. Paul says in 2 Corinthians 1:20, "For all the promises of God in him are yea, and in him Amen, unto the glory of God by us."

So don't allow yourself to be thrown off course by what your friends are saying or by what the devil is telling you, and most of all don't listen to your flesh. You have God's promises in the palm of your hands, the Bible.

Delight yourself in Him! Don't be concerned or spend all of your time focusing on how long you've been single. Spend more time enjoying your singleness. Take that time and praise God that your mate is on his way. Use that time to delight yourself in God, and He will bring your desires to pass in your life—when you least expect it. In other words, God is saying, "What you desire of Me I will give it to you!"

Your cry may be, "Lord, I want a mate, someone who is going to love me, someone I can call my own. Lord, I am tired of being by myself. Lord, I have been single for a long time. Please send me a husband/wife." The Lord's response will be, "I will. But in order for Me to grant you your request, you must delight yourself in Me first." The word *delight* in Hebrew, *anag*, means "to take great pleasure in or satisfaction in, to joy, enjoyment, or to have a strong desire." It also means "to be happy about, to make merry over."

God wants you to have a strong desire for Him, and having a strong desire for God means to put Him first in all things, doing what He wants you to do. God wants you to delight in Him before He gives you your mate. Your first obligation, however, is giving your Creator what He wants, and that is to delight in Him.

You can forfeit your blessing and what God has promised you in His Word by not delighting yourself in the Lord. When you start to complain and murmur to God, "Why don't I have anyone? All my friends are married or getting married," and start feeling sorry for yourself, you will stop the hand of God. Don't complain anymore but rejoice and be happy. Start celebrating and enjoy your singleness, and before you know it you will be married or engaged.

When you began to murmur and complain you are actually opening the door for the enemy. First Corinthians 10:10–11 says, "Neither murmur ye, as some of them also murmured, and were destroyed of the destroyer. Now all these things happened unto them for examples: and they are written for our admonition, upon whom the ends of the world are come." So the best thing to do is to rejoice; don't pay attention to time and what others are saying and doing. Your time is coming sooner than you think. If you can just wait and begin to praise God for the answer and be fully convinced that the answer is on its way, it won't be long.

Follow these simple steps, and I assure you, you cannot go wrong. God loves you above all else, and all He wants to do is bless you. The key to the blessing is to spend more time delighting and less time murmuring and complaining.

Follow James's instruction:

> But be ye doers of the word, and not hearers only, deceiving your own selves. For if any be a hearer of the word, and not a doer, he is like unto a man beholding his natural face in a glass: For he beholdeth himself, and goeth his way, and straightway forgetteth what manner of man he was. But whoso looketh into the perfect law of liberty, and continueth therein, he being not a forgetful hearer, but a doer of the work, this man shall be blessed in his deed.
>
> —JAMES 1:22–25, AMP

Scripture Reference on Delighting Thyself in the Lord

Meditate on these scriptures:

> But his delight is in the law of the Lord; and in his law doth he meditate day and night.
>
> —Psalm 1:2

> Trust in the Lord, and do good; so shalt thou dwell in the land, and verily thou shalt be fed. Delight thyself also in the Lord: and he shall give thee the desires of thine heart. Commit thy way unto the Lord; trust also in him; and he shall bring it to pass.
>
> —Psalm 37:3–5

> I will delight myself in thy statutes: I will not forget thy word.
>
> —Psalm 119:16

> Thy testimonies also are my delight and my counselors.
>
> —Psalm 119:24

> Make me to go in the path of thy commandments; for therein do I delight.
>
> —Psalm 119:35

> And I will delight myself in thy commandments, which I have loved.
>
> —Psalm 119:47

> Let thy tender mercies come unto me, that I may live: for thy law is my delight.
>
> —Psalm 119:77

I have longed for thy salvation, O Lord; and thy law is my delight.

—Psalm 119:174

I delight to do thy will, O my God: yea, thy law is within my heart.

—Psalm 40:8

For I delight in the law of God after the inward man.

—Romans 7:22

I will be glad and rejoice in thee: I will sing praise to thy name, O thou most High.

—Psalm 9:2

Let all those that seek thee rejoice and be glad in thee: and let such as love thy salvation say continually, Let God be magnified.

—Psalm 70:4

Rejoice in the Lord always: and again I say, Rejoice.

—Philippians 4:4

WORDS OF WISDOM CONCERNING DATING

As you start or venture out on finding the right mate that God has for you, let me give you some sound wisdom so that you won't be taken in by Dr. Jekyll and Mr. Hyde or some jerk or fool sent by the devil to deceive you or get you caught up into your emotion. Before we get into the words of wisdom concerning dating let's take a minute to read Proverbs. The Bible says that wisdom is the highest thing. Without wisdom you won't get very far in the dating circle. I have seen some of the smartest people get played because they didn't use wisdom and common sense. James 1:5 says, "If any of you lack wisdom, let him ask of God, that giveth to all men liberally, and upbraideth not; and it shall be given him."

Wisdom is:

- First of all, wisdom is the principal thing. The Word of God is the wisdom of God.

- The wisdom of God is the ability to discern, to comprehend, understand, to interpret, or the interpretation of spiritual matters or spiritual insight into God's plans.

- The wisdom of God is the knowledge and the ability to make the right choices at the opportune time.

- The wisdom of God also means the insight into the true nature of things. It reveals hidden things about a person's motive, heart, and character, especially our enemies'.

◙ Wisdom is not just acquiring information but practical insight with spiritual implications, knowing when and how to apply God's Word to every situation.

◙ The wisdom of God will expose the dark and secret things in our heart and mind and bring them to the surface, or light.

◙ The wisdom of God will keep people and Satan from taking advantage over you.

The proverbs of Solomon the son of David, king of Israel; To know wisdom and instruction; to perceive the words of understanding; To receive the instruction of wisdom, justice, and judgment, and equity; To give subtilty to the simple, to the young man knowledge and discretion. A wise man will hear, and will increase learning; and a man of understanding shall attain unto wise counsels: To understand a proverb, and the interpretation; the words of the wise, and their dark sayings. The fear of the LORD is the beginning of knowledge: but fools despise wisdom and instruction. My son, hear the instruction of thy father, and forsake not the law of thy mother: For they shall be an ornament of grace unto thy head, and chains about thy neck.

—PROVERBS 1:1–9

My son, if thou wilt receive my words, and hide my commandments with thee; So that thou incline thine ear unto wisdom, and apply thine heart to understanding; Yea, if thou criest after knowledge, and liftest up thy voice for understanding; If thou seekest her as silver, and searchest for her as for hid treasures; Then shalt thou understand the fear of the LORD, and find the knowledge of God. For the LORD giveth wisdom: out of his mouth cometh knowledge and understanding. He layeth up sound wisdom for the righteous: he is a buckler to them that walk uprightly. He keepeth the paths of judgment, and preserveth the way of his saints. Then shalt thou understand righteousness, and judgment, and equity; yea, every good path. When wisdom entereth into thine heart, and knowledge is pleasant unto thy soul; Discretion shall preserve thee, understanding shall keep thee: To deliver thee from the way of the evil man, from the man that speaketh froward things.

—PROVERBS 2:1–12

Happy is the man that findeth wisdom, and the man that getteth understanding. For the merchandise of it is better than the merchandise of silver, and the gain thereof than fine gold. She is more precious than rubies: and all the things thou canst desire are not to be compared unto her. Length of days is in her right hand; and in her left hand riches and honour. Her ways are ways of pleasantness, and all her paths are peace. She is a tree of life to them that lay hold upon her: and happy is every one that retaineth her. The LORD by wisdom hath founded the earth; by understanding hath he established the heavens. By his knowledge the depths are broken up, and the clouds drop down the dew. My son, let not them depart from thine eyes: keep sound wisdom and discretion: So shall they be life unto thy soul, and grace to thy neck. Then shalt thou walk in thy way safely, and thy foot shall not stumble. When thou liest down, thou shalt not be afraid: yea, thou shalt lie down, and thy sleep shall be sweet.

—PROVERBS 3:13–24

Hear, ye children, the instruction of a father, and attend to know understanding. For I give you good doctrine, forsake ye not my law. For I was my father's son, tender and only beloved in the sight of my mother. He taught me also, and said unto me, Let thine heart retain my words: keep my commandments, and live. Get wisdom, get understanding: forget it not; neither decline from the words of my mouth. Forsake her not, and she shall preserve thee: love her, and she shall keep thee. Wisdom is the principal thing; therefore get wisdom: and with all thy getting get understanding. Exalt her, and she shall promote thee: she shall bring thee to honour, when thou dost embrace her. She shall give to thine head an ornament of grace: a crown of glory shall she deliver to thee. Hear, O my son, and receive my sayings; and the years of thy life shall be many. I have taught thee in the way of wisdom; I have led thee in right paths. When thou goest, thy steps shall not be straitened; and when thou runnest, thou shalt not stumble. Take fast hold of instruction; let her not go: keep her; for she is thy life.

—PROVERBS 4:1–13

Wisdom 1

When dating always keep in mind that dating doesn't mean sex. It means courtship, the act of paying attention to that person, with the intention of developing a more intimate relationship with him or her. It is the period of a romantic relationship before marriage. In other words, you are establishing an alliance with that person to see if he or she is the one. Just because you go out on a few dates, or if he or she pays for dinner or spends all night talking on the phone, that doesn't mean that you should overlook their character. That should be the first thing—what's on their mind, their motives. Watch their behavior and their personality. Ask the most important questions first. Ask them how they feel about kids, what their view on marriage is and what commitment means to them, about God and church. A few dates are not going to cut it. You need more than a few dates with that person; a dinner and a movie is not enough.

Wisdom 2 ∞∞⤴

When dating always keep your guard up and put God and His Word first. Apply what you have learned from this book.

Wisdom 3 ∞∞⤴

When dating, be direct with that person. Let him or her know up front what you want and what you are looking for, what you expect, how you want to be treated, and that you demand respect in the relationship. If the respect is not in the relationship, nine times out of ten it won't be in the marriage.

Wisdom 4 ∞∞⤴

Find out if he or she has a hostile attitude toward the opposite sex. You want to know and investigate for yourself if this person is aggressive and intimidating. You want to find out if he or she is unsympathetic concerning your feelings, or is selfish, harsh, and argumentative in a relationship with the opposite sex.

Wisdom 5 ∞∞⤴

When dating pay close attention to see if he or she has a domineering personality. Here's how you can tell: Does he or she seem to act bossy or make all the decisions about money, what you should wear, whom you can and cannot talk to, where you should go and cannot go, controlling your every move? Does he or she treat you as his or her property? If you see these things and more, then that person has a domineering personality. Don't try to fix them; just leave them.

Wisdom 6 ⁂

This is for the men, men who have kids: Make sure that you take care of your responsibility. Running from your responsibility is not cool when you're trying to date. It is a turnoff to most women, and besides that women like and love to see men take care and spend time with their kids.

Wisdom 7 ⁂

When dating check out his or her ideas about the opposite sex. The wrong ideas about the opposite sex can and will lead to disaster in a relationship, so find out his or her ideas about the opposite sex. You will want to know what they think.

From the man's point of view, you will want to know how she thinks about a man. Is her idea of a man someone willing to be her sugar daddy, someone who can pay her bills and support her spending habits? Is she asking, What I can get from this man? My advice to you is to run as fast as you can. On the other hand, is the man's idea of a woman to be a sex object or that women are created to serve their needs only? Does he see women as equal to a man or less than a man? If the answer is less, my advice to you is to run as fast as you can.

Wisdom 8 ⁂

This is for the women, women that have kids. Men love when a woman has control over her kids. What turns men off with women who have kids is a lack of control. Men don't want to see out of control and rebellious kids; they don't like that. If you are a mother and want to date, make sure that you handle your kids and that they are respectful toward you, because it can cause problems in the relationship.

Wisdom 9 ∞∞∞

When dating be realistic in setting your goals and expectations. Don't set your goals and expectations so high that it would be impossible for someone to reach them. Remember, we are not perfect, and we do have flaws.

Wisdom 10 ∞∞∞

When dating, don't seclude yourself from people; it's not good. It's all right to get the opinion of others, especially if they are your friends who have your best interests at heart. Be open-minded with others when they voice their opinion and in what they see and tell you about that person. Don't have the attitude the he or she wants them for themselves. Receive and think about what they have said and keep your eyes open, or just pray on it.

Wisdom 11 ∞∞∞

Spend more time dating in open areas or in public places where there are lots of people. Try not to spend too much of your time alone, especially at your place and his or her place. You don't want to give place to the flesh. Spend more time praying and in the Word or around friends who are Christians that hold the same values (purity).

Wisdom 12 ∞∞∞

When dating find out how much he or she loves God. Find out, does he or she love the Lord thy God with all of their heart, soul, mind, body, strength, money, and all of his or her material possessions? If they love God that way, he or she should be able through Christ to love you that way.

Wisdom 13 ✄✄✄⊙

Make sure that he or she knows the difference between love and lust. What people call love is actually lust. This is how you can tell: love always gives at its own expense without any hidden motive.

First Corinthians 13:4–8 is a perfect example of love:

> Love endures long and is patient and kind; love never is envious nor boils over with jealousy, is not boastful or vainglorious, does not display itself haughtily. It is not conceited (arrogant and inflated with pride); it is not rude (unmannerly) and does not act unbecomingly. Love (God's love in us) does not insist on its own rights or its own way, for it is not self-seeking; it is not touchy or fretful or resentful; it takes no account of the evil done to it [it pays no attention to a suffered wrong].It does not rejoice at injustice and unrighteousness, but rejoices when right and truth prevail. Love bears up under anything and everything that comes, is ever ready to believe the best of every person, its hopes are fadeless under all circumstances, and it endures everything [without weakening]. Love never fails [never fades out or becomes obsolete or comes to an end]. As for prophecy (the gift of interpreting the divine will and purpose), it will be fulfilled and pass away; as for tongues, they will be destroyed and cease; as for knowledge, it will pass away [it will lose its value and be superseded by truth]. (AMP)

Lust is when you try to get things at other people's expense, having a wrong motive for doing things.

Wisdom 14 ∞∞∞⊚

Ladies, don't run behind or pursue a man. That's not your job; that's the man's job. Just make yourself available.

> He who finds a [true] wife finds a good thing, and
> obtaineth favor from the Lord.
> —PROVERBS 18:22

Wisdom 15 ∞∞∞⊚

Set boundaries. Be careful of how much time you spend alone. Be careful not to indulge in heavy kissing and touching, because it can lead to sexual intercourse.

Wisdom 16 ∞∞∞⊚

Don't look at being lonely as a negative thing. Look at it as an opportunity for preparation. Use that time to get yourself together, to work on some stuff. Maybe God is dealing with you concerning your attitude, your finances, housekeeping, spending more time in the Word and in prayer, your health, your insecurities. Whatever it is that needs to be dealt with, take that time and allow God to work on you.

Wisdom 17 ∞∞∞⊚

Never go into a relationship with old baggage. What happened in your past relationship or marriage, let it stay there. If you are not healed from your past, it is best not to get involved or even think about dating until you are completely healed.

Wisdom 18 ∞∞∞⊚

When dating never put yourself in a compromising situation or compromise your standard. Never reveal or talk

SEVEN SIMPLE STEPS OF FINDING A MATE GOD'S WAY

about deep and personal stuff too soon, like personal finance or a future together, because she or he might not be the one.

Wisdom 19

Never think for a second that marriage is the answer for loneliness. If you do you will be separated, or you will end up in divorce court. Marriage is not the cure for loneliness, nor does it provide the answer for low self-worth, depression, and security.

Wisdom 20

You must use common sense and mix it with your spirituality or spiritual maturity when you decide to date.

Wisdom 21

Never be in a rush to get into a relationship. Just take your time and trust God. Isaiah 28:16 says, "Therefore thus saith the Lord God, Behold, I lay in Zion for a foundation a stone, a tried stone, a precious corner stone, a sure foundation: he that believeth shall not make haste." The Hebrew word for "haste" is *chuwsh*, which means "to act quickly, to hurry."

Wisdom 22

When dating or pursuing a mate always remember your PFP, which stands for prayer, fasting, and patience. The Bible says that we are to always pray and to pray without ceasing. Not only should you pray but also fast. Jesus prayed and fasted all night long concerning who should be His twelve disciples. Throughout the Bible people fasted in order to hear from God concerning their situation. Fasting will help keep the flesh down so that it won't get in the way of what God is doing in you. And don't forget about patience. James 1:4 says, "But let patience have her perfect work, that ye may be perfect and entire, wanting nothing." The word *patience* means "to remain the same until your situation changes." In other words, continue doing what you were doing until it manifests.

Wisdom 23 ∞∞₀

Always remember that love is kind. No matter what happens we must walk and show love, but trust is not something you give. It must be earned. Always show love and be very honest when things are not working out. Let him or her know that you want to end this relationship. Be kind and gentle about it.

Wisdom 24 ∞∞₀

Make sure that they respect your assignment from God. If they don't respect your assignment, you know what to do. Cut him or her off as soon as possible.

Wisdom 25 ∞∞₀

When dating make purity your number one, top priority. Let that word, *purity*, be on your mind, heart, and always before the Lord when dating. It is so easy to get sidetracked with others things such as looks, insecurity, lust, and charm, and end up with a used body, a guilty conscience, pregnancy, and a broken heart.

Wisdom 26 ∞∞₀

This is for the women: When dating pay close attention to his work habits. Find out how long he has been working on his job and how many jobs he had in the last five years. That says a lot about a person. If he had three or more jobs in the last five years, it is a bad sign. It shows a lack of stability. Watch how he treats and talks to his mother. If he talks to his mother like she's a child it is a bad sign, because he is going to talk to you the same way he talks to his mother. You don't want to get involved with a man who is lazy or a mama's boy, where the mother does everything for him and she is quick to defend him. You should want a man who is more independent and knows how to put his mother in check in a nice, godly way. If he runs to his mother for everything, especially when you get into a disagreement, that's a bad sign, ladies. Remember, ladies, you cannot turn a mama's boy, a lazy man, and a player into a man or a husband.

Ladies, due to the fact that girls mature faster than boys, choosing a man is like choosing a fruit. When I was a young boy my mother used to take me to the supermarket, or we would stop at a fruit stand where people sell fruit on the sidewalk. She would pick up the fruit and look at it for a long time. Then she would put it back. To me the fruit looked fine or good. Then I would ask her why she put the fruit back. She would say, "Because it wasn't mature yet," meaning it wasn't ripe or fully developed. It was picked before its time. That's the way with these women. They pick guys before their time, and now they are angry and frustrated in the relationship. Don't get angry or be frustrated. Just send him back home to his mother.

Wisdom 27

This is for the ladies: how to recognize the signs of an immature man and a mama's boy. Let's start with the immature man first. He may have a child or make babies, but he runs from his responsibility of being a father and helping the mother to raise their children.

He would rather play video games, watch TV, and be on the Internet all day and night than socialize with others and get a job. He cannot and will not commit to anything and still lives at home with his parents. He works at a minimum-wage job just to support his habits. He is lazy and won't look for a job, and is sitting at home being a couch potato.

Mommy is doing his laundry, cooking, cleaning, and paying the neighbor to do the yard while he is in the house watching TV, listening to music, and not paying any bills to help out.

He loves to party and expects his parent to do everything for him, including paying his bills.

He thinks that he is God's gift to women.

He is still trying to find himself and does not have or know his own identity.

He is leaning on his mother (or father) a little too much (co-dependency).

He won't support himself.

He lives off his own ego and self-pleasure, which often leads to self-admiration and self-centeredness. He is selfish and conceited.

He remains in a rebellious stage of life, always making up excuses why he can't do this or that.

He is always blaming other people for his problems or why he can't get ahead.

He cannot or does not know how to form a real and meaningful relationship (with the opposite sex).

He is incapable of adjusting to any of society's norms or values. (In other words, you can't go anywhere with him in public functions or settings without him making a fool out of himself or acting like a jerk, always wanting to be seen.)

He sits back and watches things happen instead of making thing happen.

He's stuck in his only little world and not open to the opinions of those people trying to help him.

He's mad at you and the world because his parents stop supporting him financially.

He uses anger and violence to solve his problems or when you two are in a disagreement.

He is always running from his responsibilities and not stepping up to the plate.

Ladies, beware if he always has to be told what to do and never or barely takes the initiative to do things.

Be careful if he has others taking care of his responsibilities.

With the mama's boys, ladies, you must remember that it is important that guys treat their mother with much love and great respect, and that is a good thing. On the other hand, some guys never learn how to draw the line of cutting the apron string. Of course we (especially the men) blame the mother for not allowing her son to put some emotional distance and balance between their relationship when he was growing up. No woman in this world can instill in a boy or a young man what a real man can because it is not in a woman's DNA to do so, and that is the same with a man concerning his daughter. It has been said that the majority of women (especially single women) raise their girls and pamper their boys, and now the girls and the ladies of this generation are wondering where the real men are.

The signs of a mama's boy are:

- Always seeking his mother's approval.

- Always putting his mother in your business.

- Whenever you have a disagreement, he calls his mother for advice and then tells you what she says.

- Always putting his mother before you.

- Refusing to stand up to his mother when it comes down to you.

- He wants you to look like his mother.

- He wants you to act like his mother.

- He wants you to cook for him like his mother.

- He wants you to dress like his mother.

- He doesn't like to be away from his mother for a long period of time.

- He wants you to clean up behind him like his mother.

- He wants you to treat him like how his mother treated him.

- His mother is always defending him and she knows he is wrong.

- He values his mother's opinion more than yours.

- He is well over his adult years and still calls his mother "Mommy."

- He has his mother's name or a picture of her face tattooed on his body.

- He has never planned to move out from his mother's house or never makes any plans to do so.

- He puts his mother in the front seat of the car and you in the back.

- He admits that he won't enter into a serious relationship with anyone that his mother doesn't approve of first.

- He wants you to do everything for him and take charge of the situation.

- He is always calling and texting his mother when he's out on a date with you. (One time is acceptable, but it must be quick.)

- His mother is always justifying his behavior and not calling what you see in him like it is.

- He wants you to smell like his mother (e.g., her perfume).

SEVEN SIMPLE STEPS OF FINDING A MATE GOD'S WAY

- He puts his mother on a pedestal and compliments her more than you.

- He seems to be a little more feminine than masculine—that doesn't necessary mean that he is gay, but it may mean he has more of his mother's upbringing in him or that he has been raised more around women in his family, like sisters or aunts, than a male or his father.

- You hear his mother constantly saying, "That's my baby."

- He is always seeking advice from his mother that only a man can give him.

- He is always up under his mother.

- He is always up under you, following you around from room to room like he does his mother.

Wisdom 28

This is for the man: Don't be fooled by her looks and her body. Pay attention to how she dresses. Does she wear revealing clothes, or does she dress more conservatively but stylish? Watch how she spends her money. Does she spend her money wisely or foolishly? Remember, men, you cannot turn a ghetto woman or a loose woman into a housewife. Instead of going out to eat all the time, let her cook sometimes to see if she can cook, and visit her apartment or house to see how well she keeps her place. Is it nice and clean, or is it dirty? That says a lot about her. It is the little things that will make a difference.

Wisdom 29

One of the main things you would want to keep your eyes on is how well he or she does under pressure, when things are not going right. Do they lose their temper, break things, throw things, get ready to fight, or are they willing to talk like a mature adult and handle things according to the Word of God? If the answer is "losing their temper, breaking things, throwing things, and getting ready to fight," don't go any farther. Leave that man or that woman right where they're at. Tell him or her to lose your number.

Wisdom 30

Before you decide to date, be secure in yourself and in God. Love yourself first before you can love anyone else, and be confident that God loves you when others don't. When others reject you or overlook you, know that God has accepted you just the way you are. Remember these scriptures that will help you to overcome your insecurity.

> Having predestinated us unto the adoption of children by Jesus Christ to himself, according to the good pleasure of his will, To the praise of the glory of his grace, wherein he hath made us accepted in the beloved.
> —EPHESIANS 1:5–6

> When my father and my mother forsake me, then the LORD will take me up.
> —PSALM 27:10

> For thou hast possessed my reins: thou hast covered me in my mother's womb. I will praise thee; for I am fearfully and wonderfully made: marvellous are thy works; and that my soul knoweth right well.
> —PSALM 139:13–14

How precious also are thy thoughts unto me, O God! how great is the sum of them!

—Psalm 139:17

Many, O Lord my God, are thy wonderful works which thou hast done, and thy thoughts which are to us-ward: they cannot be reckoned up in order unto thee: if I would declare and speak of them, they are more than can be numbered.

—Psalm 40:5, amp

For I know the thoughts that I think toward you, saith the Lord, thoughts of peace, and not of evil, to give you an expected end.

—Jeremiah 29:11

Wisdom 31 ﹊﹊﹊

Remember that insecurity is a doorway to the enemy. It opens the door to abuse. It will cause you to lower your standards, to compromise, to feel judged by other people's opinions and what they said and think about you. It will cause you to become a people pleaser more than a God pleaser. It will cause to lose your identity and take on someone else's identity. Insecurity will make you feel that you're not good enough, pretty enough, and smart enough, always feeling inadequate. This is not the will of God for your life. Overcome these things before you look for a mate.

Wisdom 32 ﹊﹊﹊

Ladies, when dating or seeking a mate these are the qualities that you would like to see in him and pray about:

- A Moses, with the ability to hear from God to lead and guide.

- A David, a man that is after God's own heart, a man who knows how to praise and worship God.

- A Daniel, a man of prayer and integrity.

- A Joseph, a man who knows how to run from sin, especially sexual sin.

- A Solomon, a man of godly wisdom.

- An Isaiah, a man who knows how to speak a word over your life and into your life.

- An Abraham, a man of faith.

- A Paul, a man who has revelation, understanding, and knowledge of God's Holy Word that can feed into your life without putting you into bondage and using the Word for his self-gain.

Most of all he must be like Jesus Christ our Lord, a man of a pure, unconditional love, sacrifice, mercy, power, patience, kindness, meekness, willingness to forgive, tenderness, long-suffering, and constancy; someone who will cover, protect, provide for, and be able to minister to you with grace.

Wisdom 33

Men, when dating or seeking a mate, these are the qualities that you would like to see in her and pray about:

- A Sarah, a woman of great faith, a loving and a committed wife.

- An Abigail, a woman of quick wisdom and generosity.

- An Anna, a woman who serves God faithfully day and night.

- A Deborah, a prophetess, a woman who knows how to speak God's Word over your life and into your life.

- A Dorcas, a woman of good works and charitable deeds.

- A Ruth, a woman of determination and faithfulness.

- A Hannah, a woman of a powerful prayer life and faithfulness in keeping her promise and commitment to God.

- An Esther, a woman of beauty, very graceful, marked by poise, dignity, and politeness.

Take heed, men, to King Lemuel's mother's advice in Proverbs 31:10–31 about what to look for in a woman. She doesn't have to be perfect, fine, and shaped like an hourglass, but she must be virtuous, which means she must have or show moral goodness and righteousness with moral integrity.

> Who can find a virtuous woman? for her price is far above rubies. The heart of her husband doth safely trust in her, so that he shall have no need of spoil.

This is the first characteristic of a virtuous woman, that her husband or her husband-to-be can safely trust in her. He can trust her with the household affairs, he can trust her in all of her business dealings, that she knows how to make wise financial decisions. He knows she will not work deceitfully but will be a true partner and helpmeet to him. In other words, she won't take the money and buy a new dress when the light bill is due or go on a shopping spree when bills are due.

> She will do him good and not evil all the days of her life.

This is the second characteristic of a virtuous woman. She will never speak evil of him behind his back, especially to her girlfriends or tear him down with her mouth, and she doesn't make life or working together difficult for him. She will not willfully do anything that may damage his reputation, family, and the estate. She will do him good all the days of her life by providing what is fit for him in health and in sickness and when times are hard. She will use her mouth to speak words of kindness over him, not words of death.

> She seeketh wool, and flax, and worketh willingly with her hands. She is like the merchants' ships; she bringeth her food from afar. She riseth also while it is yet night, and giveth meat to her household, and a portion to her maidens. She considereth a field, and buyeth it: with the fruit of her hands she planteth a vineyard. She girdeth her loins with strength, and strengtheneth her arms. She perceiveth that her merchandise is good: her candle goeth not out by night. She layeth her hands to the spindle, and her hands hold the distaff.

This is the third characteristic of a virtuous woman. She is not lazy. She is willing to work.

> She stretcheth out her hand to the poor; yea, she reacheth forth her hands to the needy.

This is the fourth characteristic of a virtuous woman. She reaches out to the poor and needy with sympathy and readiness to help those that are oppressed by misfortunes.

> She is not afraid of the snow for her household: for all her household are clothed with scarlet. She maketh herself coverings of tapestry; her clothing is silk and purple. Her husband is known in the gates,

when he sitteth among the elders of the land. She
maketh fine linen, and selleth it; and delivereth gir-
dles unto the merchant. Strength and honour are
her clothing; and she shall rejoice in time to come.

This is the fifth characteristic of a virtuous woman. She is
always thinking of and planning ahead for her family.

She openeth her mouth with wisdom; and in her
tongue is the law of kindness.

This is the sixth characteristic of a virtuous woman. She
is always giving guidance and instruction to those who will
listen. She never gossips, she never slanders, and she is never
hasty or "passionate," meaning "compelled by, or ruled by
intense emotion or strong feeling." She is firm but very gentle.

She looketh well to the ways of her household, and
eateth not the bread of idleness.

This is the seventh characteristic of a virtuous woman.
She manages or watches over her household affairs first by
putting her family first, not her friends and other people
first, especially her mother and her other family members.
She instructs her children not to eat the bread of idleness,
meaning teaching them not to be lazy.

Her children arise up, and call her blessed; her husband also, and he praiseth her. Many daughters have
done virtuously, but thou excellest them all. Favour
is deceitful, and beauty is vain: but a woman that
feareth the LORD, she shall be praised. Give her of
the fruit of her hands; and let her own works praise
her in the gates.

A PRAYER/CONFESSION
FOR THE RIGHT MATE

Heavenly Father, Your Word says in Philippians 4:6, "Be careful for nothing; but in every thing by prayer and supplication with thanksgiving let your requests be made known unto God." Father, You said that it is not good for us to be alone and that You have created man and woman to be together as one. Lord, lead me to the one You have chosen and created just for me. While I wait for You to reveal Your will in this matter, help me to work on me. Help me to address those things that are in my life that can hinder me from being all that I can be in You and the one You have for me.

Help me to stay focused on You as I wait. Don't let my mind be consumed with finding a mate but finding Your perfect will for my life. You say to seek first the kingdom of God and all these things should be added unto me. Lord, I thank You for my wonderful mate, someone who is saved and filled with the Spirit, who delights in Your commandments. Lord, I thank You for a mate that is full of the Word, faith, wisdom, and character, someone who is a tither and a doer of the Word, and most of all full of the love of God. In Jesus' name I pray. Amen.

Once you have prayed this prayer, start confessing the Word until it comes to pass.

Lord, I confess that my mate is on his/her way. Lord, I thank You for my mate, who is filled with the Holy Ghost and wisdom and functions as a true man/woman of God. Lord, I believe and receive by faith that the one You have for me is here with me now by faith according to Mark 11:23–25. Father, by faith I receive her/him into my life now in Jesus' name. I refuse to talk death, doubt, and unbelief. Father, there are good men/women out there to be taking, and I thank You for mine, in Jesus' name. Amen.

Keep confessing it every day until it comes to pass in your life.

Death and life are in the power of the tongue: and they that love it shall eat the fruit thereof.

—PROVERBS 18:21

RECAP

Establishing Your Foundation

Write in your own words what you have learned from this chapter and how you can apply it to your own personal life.

_____

_____

_____

Acknowledge God When Seeing a Mate

Write in your own words what you have learned from this chapter and how you can apply it to your own personal life.

_____

_____

_____

Put All Your Time and Energy Into Seeking God, Then a Mate

Write in your own words what you have learned from this chapter and how you can apply it to your own personal life.

_____

_____

_____

Watch the Fruit That Is Being Produced in Their Lives

Write in your own words what you have learned from this chapter and how you can apply it to your own personal life.

_____

_____

_____

Don't Seek an Unbeliever (Non-Christian) for a Mate

Write in your own words what you have learned from this chapter and how you can apply it to your own personal life.

_____

_____

_____

Being Led by the Spirit, Not Your Flesh

Write in your own words what you have learned from this chapter and how you can apply it to your own personal life.

_____

_____

_____

DELIGHT YOURSELF IN THE LORD

Write in your own words what you have learned from this chapter and how you can apply it to your own personal life.

_____

_____

_____

A PRAYER FOR SALVATION AND THE BAPTISM OF THE HOLY SPIRIT

Heavenly Father, You said in John 6:37 that he that cometh to You, You will in no wise cast out. You also said in Acts 2:21, "Whosoever shall call on the name of the Lord shall be saved." Lord, I am calling on Your name. I pray and ask Jesus to come into my heart and be my Lord. Father, I acknowledge that I am a sinner, born in sin.

Lord, You said in Romans 10:9–10, "That if thou shalt confess with thy mouth the Lord Jesus, and shalt believe in thine heart that God hath raised him from the dead, thou shalt be saved. For with the heart man believeth unto righteousness; and with the mouth confession is made unto salvation." Father God, I believe that Jesus is Lord and that He was raised from the dead for me, and I ask Him to come into my heart and life now, in Jesus' name. I now confess that I am saved, a child of the living God.

How to Receive the Baptism of the Holy Spirit

Father, I am now born again, born of the Spirit. I am a Christian, a child of almighty God. I am saved. You also said in Your Word, "If ye then, being evil, know how to give good gifts unto your children: how much more shall your heavenly Father give the Holy Spirit to them that ask him?" (Luke 11:13). Father, I am asking You to fill me with the Holy

Spirit, the evidence of speaking in tongues. Holy Spirit, rise up within me, as I praise God. I fully expect to speak with other tongues as the Spirit gives me utterance (Acts 2:4).

Now begin to praise God for filling you with the Holy Spirit by faith. Speak the words and syllables you receive, not in your own language but in the language given to you by the leading of the Holy Spirit. You have to be willing to use your own voice; God will not force you to speak. Begin to worship and praise Him in your heavenly language (other tongues).

ABOUT THE AUTHOR

GREGORY BACKMON LIVES in Orangeburg, South Carolina, with his wife, Ghislaine Backmon, along with their four children and one grandchild.

Gregory Backmon received the call of God over fifteen years ago to teach the Word of God to believers for the upbuilding of the kingdom of God. Elder Backmon is a firm believer of increased faith through Scripture-based confessions. With a strong emphasis on intercessory prayer and faith confessions he teaches how we can live victoriously in this earth by exercising the authority given to us as children of God in our inheritance based on us receiving the Lord Jesus Christ as our Lord and Savior. He teaches spiritual principles for maintaining victory in daily situations, knowing we are world overcomers through Christ our Lord.

His vision from the Lord is based on Acts 26:16–18:

> But rise, and stand upon thy feet: for I have appeared unto thee for this purpose, to make thee a minister and a witness both of these things which thou hast seen, and of those things in the which I will appear unto thee; Delivering thee from the people, and from the Gentiles, unto whom now I send thee, To open their eyes, and to turn them from darkness to light, and from the power of Satan unto God, that they may receive forgiveness of sins, and inheritance among them which are sanctified by faith that is in me.

Elder Backmon continues to press on to teach and manifest God's power for divine living in love, faith, deliverance, healing, and prosperity by applying basic Scripture principles to our everyday life for the walk in God's "greater light."

CONTACT THE AUTHOR

E-MAIL:

gregorybackmon@att.net